Beach Reflections

Jennifer Clymer Harris

WestBow Press books may be ordered through booksellers or by contacting:

WestBow Press
A Division of Thomas Nelson & Zondervan
1663 Liberty Drive
Bloomington, IN 47403
www.westbowpress.com
1 (866) 928-1240

Because of the dynamic nature of the Internet, any web addresses or links contained in this book may have changed since publication and may no longer be valid. The views expressed in this work are solely those of the author and do not necessarily reflect the views of the publisher, and the publisher hereby disclaims any responsibility for them.

Any people depicted in stock imagery provided by Getty Images are models, and such images are being used for illustrative purposes only. Certain stock imagery © Getty Images.

ISBN: 978-1-9736-2033-4 (sc)
ISBN: 978-1-9736-2034-1 (e)

Library of Congress Control Number: 2018902385

Print information available on the last page.

WestBow Press rev. date: 6/18/2018

Beach Reflections

My life and this book are dedicated to Abba Father, who made me so much more than an "eight cow wife." I'm elated to share some of the life lessons I experienced when I lived in paradise, Amelia Island, Florida. I hope you can relate and use your senses to imagine that you are at your favorite beach.

If not...

A beach awaits you to stimulate your mind, refresh your body, and renew your spirit.
    A million reasons to stay home? I don't want to hear it!

You'll fill your cup overflowing
    and many times without knowing,

your thoughts will wander
    way back yonder.

To the beach, to relive the days that made you smile,
    if even for a while.

When you return home from the beach, instead of just a shell in your pocket and
    sand in your shoes,
        you'll have a treasure chest of sweet memories so you won't have the blues!

JUMP(Jen Under Master Plan)

Lala Sue Clymer (May 17, 1926 – February 24, 2013)

Ma Sue, today you've been gone a year.
    I've held you in my heart, oh so dear.
        Your face is fading, I do fear.
            I've missed you so much, you own my every tear.

Our separation has been harder than I thought.
I'm created, being made up of everything that you taught.
I am wearing clothing and jewelry that you bought
surrounded by yard sale "prizes" that you sought.

How could I not think of you every hour?
Your love carries so much power.

You are so alive within all of us.
I know you wouldn't want your family to make all this fuss.

Tell Daddy, "hey."
We'll be there someday.
I bet you are eating so many sweets,
that you can't stand on your little feets!

A new body - no meds
and you don't have to wear those TEDS!

Mom, I saw the moment you looked toward
Jesus and what overwhelming peace.
I knew then that death was a gentle release.

From suffering and pain,
to your heavenly reward you did gain.

I have such gratitude to have had you as my mom.
When I think of you I close my eyes,
take a deep breath,
and feel such calm.

JUMP

"For your Maker is your husband - the Lord Almighty is His name." Isaiah 54:5 (NIV) [1]

Several years ago a friend told me the story of *Johnny Lingo & the Eight-Cow Wife.* [2] He was known as the sharpest trader on several Pacific Islands but quite the fool for paying money just to buy a plain, skinny wife. Who would do such a foolish thing? None of them! Sarita was pale and had matted hair. She walked with her head down and shoulders rounded. She had poor self-esteem. Her father had resigned himself to accept just one cow. Johnny knew Sarita believed she was nothing. When he paid more than was ever offered for any other woman on the Islands without negotiation, she sees her worth in his eyes. The result was amazing. Sarita became the most beautiful woman: erect posture, sparkling eyes, beaming with happiness reflecting the value her husband had put in her, all because of what he paid for her.

Psalm 50:10 tells us our God owns every animal of the forest and the cattle on a thousand hills. But when He looked into our eyes, He knew we felt worthless like Sarita. Payment for us of eight cows or cattle on a thousand hills wouldn't do. We needed to see his love. "For God so loved the world that he gave his only and unique Son so that everyone who trusts in him may have eternal life, instead of being utterly destroyed. For God did not send the Son into the world to judge the world, but rather so that through him, the world might be saved." John 3:16-17 (Complete Jewish Bible) [3]

Jesus paid more than was ever sacrificed for every man, woman, and child who has ever lived without negotiation. His love for us held him on the cross so we can live. "Greater love has no one than this, that he lay down his life for his friends." John 15:13 (NIV) How much more valued can I be?

My prayer is that I could only see myself as God sees me. Then, I would move closer and closer to the image of his precious Son Jesus.

"And I am sure of this: that the One who began a good work among you will keep it growing until it is completed on the day of the Messiah Yeshua (Christ Jesus)." Philippians 1:6 (Complete Jewish Bible)

Be Lord of my life today -

ruler of my heart

and mind.

I invite you to forever stay.

Let your glow show.

May I be your hands

and feet

to all I meet,

because I know your way

is so very neat!

Amen.

JUMP

(Use of hand gestures for this morning
prayer has made it more meaningful to me.)

She Who Loves the Beach

No words can express
the depth of her contentment
as she walks along the beach.
As the waves lap against the shores
they create the rhythm of her life.
The scent of salty air
is perfume to her senses
and the sounds of the beach
are a melodic symphony
to her ears.
As the balmy breezes
kiss her sun-bronzed skin,
she wonders…
could there ever be
a greater destiny
than to be born with a love
for the treasures of the sea?
Here, she is home.

© Suzy Toronto
www.suzytoronto.com

Suzy Toronto [4]

Beach Proverbs For Sharing

"I hope you will put up with a little of my foolishness;
but you are already doing that." 2 Corinthians 11:1 (NIV)

1. "And God said, 'Let the water under the sky be gathered to one place,
and let dry ground appear.' And it was so. God called the dry ground
'land,' and the gathered waters he called 'sea.' "And God saw that it was
good." Genesis 1:9-10 (NIV)

"Kissed by the Sun" by Doug Cavanah[5]

2. "The sea, once it casts its spell, holds one in its net of wonder forever." Jacques Cousteau

3. Smile when you crunch sand between your teeth and remember where you've been.

4.   Don't get irritated when you find sand embedded in your bar of soap. Just think of the exfoliation.

5.   What do aging and thongs have in common with the ocean?
     They both "creep" up on you like the high tide.

6.   What washes up on really small beaches?
     Microwaves

7.   There are times in our lives when we have to just go for it like the sea gulls. Set your target. Dive head first at an accelerated speed down into uncertain waters. Bingo! Just sometimes we get lucky.

8. "You can never cross the ocean unless you have the courage to lose sight of the shore." Christopher Columbus (1451-1506)

"The sea is the same as it has been since before men ever went on it in boats." Ernest Hemmingway (1899-1961)

"Ships that pass in the night, and speak each other in passing, only a signal shown, and a distant voice in the darkness; So on the ocean of life, we pass and speak one another, only a look and a voice, then darkness again and a silence." Henry Wadsworth Longfellow (1807-1882)

9. Come to the sea, and your spirit will be set free.

10. You can apply so much "Son" block that you don't benefit from the vitamin D (deliverance). "Let the Sonshine in." The color in your cheeks will do a body good.

11. Be still. Close your eyes. *Feel* the cool breeze tassel your hair and lightly massage your body. *Hear* the rhythmic waves roar as if to wash your cares away. *Smell* the salty air intermingled with the scent of coconut suntan lotion. Open your eyes to *view* a never-ending body of water that reaches as far as other continents. Watch boats bobbing on the horizon. See joyful people of all ages smiling, whether they're walking holding hands, kicking water at the ocean's edge, jogging, or just being still to snag a few shark teeth. You will see families celebrating life, building sand castles, building relationships, playing with their dogs, babies eating sand, dolphins dancing, seagulls soaring, and white foam tickling your feet as you dig your toes deeper into the warm sand to avoid a crashing wave. Appreciate the brevity of sandcastles. The ocean experience involves all your senses.

"Taste and see that the Lord is good." Psalms 34:8 (NIV)

"Every good and perfect gift is from above." James 1:17 (NIV)

12. Some sea treasures, like my prized purple and orange star fish stolen by a seagull while floating in a cup of water, are meant to be enjoyed for a short while. Enjoy treasures while you can, because such joys can be taken away prematurely, and memories will be all that remains to hold in our hearts and minds.

13. Sometimes you miss part of something important when you search for sea treasures and only a little bit is peeking out, or perhaps you see the shape of what might be under the surface. It takes faith to see with spiritual eyes what's not yet been revealed.

14. Sometimes you reach out and grab a sea treasure and don't know if it's a perfect one until you wash it off in the waves. We need to be washed in the cleansing flow of the "Perfect One" for us to be a keeper.

15. Orangish pink sunsets are breathtaking every time and occur so fast that talking during a sunset seems unreligious or unappreciative. I am guilty. I missed it. I repent.

"The Sea, For Me, Is Where I Long To Be." Brandi Fitzgerald

16. Don't get a pedicure before going to the beach. It's a waste of money because the polish chips and walking on the sand removes calluses anyway.

17. Don't walk on the edge of the water with a cell phone. Even a calm sea can hide a wave that carries a punch and knocks you on your fanny. Dead cell phone. May be a subliminal message. If you are distracted by jabber on your cell while at the beach, then the main thing isn't the main thing.

18. You can't walk near the edge of the water without getting wet. You can't play with temptation for very long without getting drawn into sin.

19. Brown fat looks better than white fat.

20. Somehow walking to collect shells, sea glass, shark teeth, and critters doesn't seem like exercise.

21. The best treasures are from the sea, not the mall.

"Benched Beach Basket of Treasures" by Rhonda McEnroe www.ENROE.studio.com 270-993-2282 [6]

22. Treasures from the sea are free.

23. **Advice from Sea gathered from various coastal signs:**

Live deep

Come out of your Shell

Take time to Coast

Avoid Pier Pressure

Make Waves

Expand your Horizon

Let Worries Drift Away

Be Shore of Yourself

Don't get Tied Down

Don't be Crabby

Seas Every Opportunity

Whale, Hello there

24. **Irish blessing**

"I wish you health, I wish you well, and happiness galore.

I wish you luck for you and friends; what could I wish you more?

May your joys be as deep as the oceans, your troubles as light as its foam.

And may you find, sweet peace of mind, wherever you may roam." Author Unknown

25. Every day at Amelia Island is a good day.

26. Food tastes better when eaten outdoors.

"Frolic" by Danny Phifer [7]

27. **frolic** - full of fun; to make merry; to play and run about happily (Webster's New Collegiate Dictionary) [8]

"A child's world is fresh and new and beautiful, full of wonder and excitement. It is our misfortune that for most of us that clear–eyed vision, that true instinct for what is beautiful and awe-inspiring, is dimmed and even lost before we reach adulthood." Rachel Carson

28. Nemo is a hero to most children. Children readily see that he has one large fin and one smaller fin, yet he has a "can do" attitude. My granddaughter would smile and say, "Nemo's not perfect; I'm not perfect; Mimi's not perfect."

But the Lord said to Samuel, "Do not consider his appearance or his height... The Lord does not look at the things people look at. People look at the outward appearance, but the Lord looks at the heart." 1 Samuel 16:7 (NIV)

"Praise the Lord from all the earth...and all ocean depths." Psalm 148:6-8 (NIV)

Annie Clymer Coleman[9]

29. "He has made everything beautiful in its time." Ecclesiastes 3:11 (NIV)

Photo by Sandra Morrison, Amelia Island, Florida[10]

Painting by Hannah Haunte, Age 8[11]

30. "Either you decide to stay in the shallow end of the pool or you go out in the ocean." –Christopher Reeve (1952-2004)

31. I enjoy watching other people fly kites. I get the benefit without being "tied down." Kind of like I enjoy the end result of people fishing without having to sit still long enough to catch a fish.

32. It's acceptable to act like a kid at the beach.

33. It's easier to connect with complete strangers on the beach. I've met the nicest people during beach walks. Maybe they wouldn't be as nice in their stressed-out work environments. Perhaps I wouldn't be either, but the beach helps all of us in being nicer people.

34. "Dear Ocean, Thank you for making us feel tiny, humble, inspired and salty . . . all at once." Author Unknown

35. "Command those… to put their hope in God, who richly provides us with everything for our enjoyment." 1 Timothy 6:17 (NIV)

Photo by Edna Roeder 912-441-0107[12]

36. Saving as many starfish as you can by offering them back to their mother ocean is a grand humanitarian act. You can't save them all, but it's oh, so worth it to the ones you gently toss back in the water.

37.   Sharks spoil the fun! Where there are shark teeth, there are gums!

Photo by Valerie Tipton[13]

38. If I saw "Flipper" in the sea while I was swimming, I'd probably "flip out".

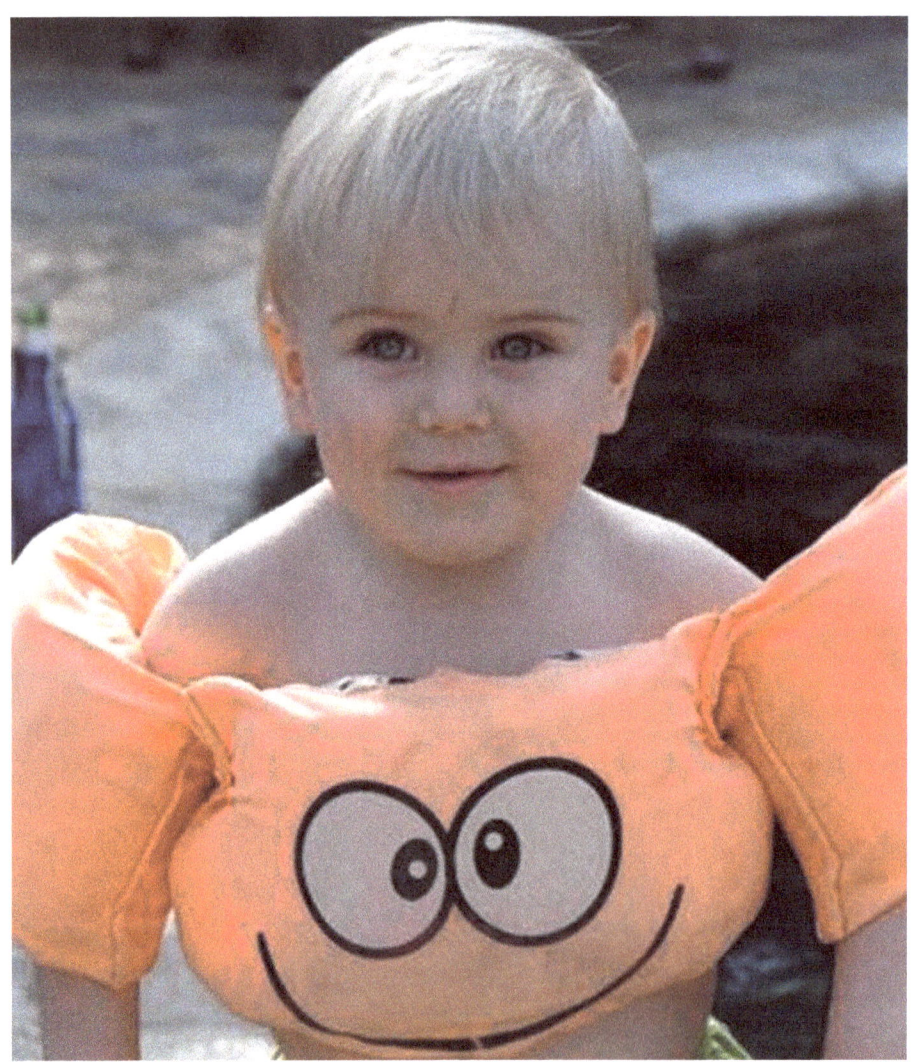

39. Like life, begin your beach walk headed into a nor'easter. At the end of your journey, you'll need the wind at your back.

40. In Florida, flip-flops are not seasonal.

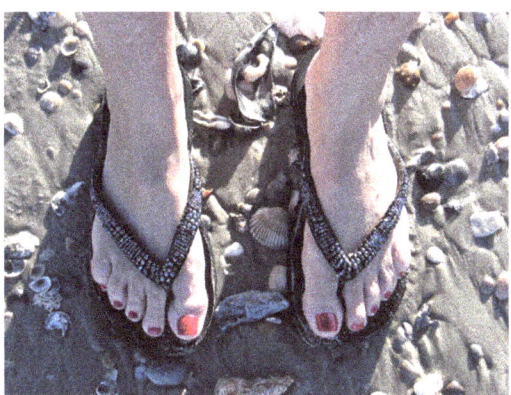

41. There is such a thing as a flip-flop wardrobe.

42. In Florida, a bad-hair day is the norm.

43. In Florida, what's makeup? See how much money I've saved on blush!

44. "A drop in the ocean,
    A change in the weather,
    I was praying that you and me
    Might end up together." Ron Pope

45. Beach bonfires are the best.

46. Someday God will tell me how many grains of sand and how many stars there are.

(Sing to the tune "When You Wish Upon A Star")
When your hope is in the Lord,
Makes no difference who you are.
Anything within His will,
Your dreams come true.

(JUMP)

47. Like God, the ocean is always there. We may turn away and leave for a day or a year, but God and the ocean are always constant, faithful, and welcome us back each time. We can trust their nature; they never change and are always the same yesterday, today, and forever.

48.   The ocean quiets my soul more than a massage, a soak in a hot tub, or a glass of wine. For a hyperactive person, the gift of relaxation and a sense of peace are rare treasures.

49. The mysterious marsh draws us with its "here today, gone tomorrow" mirage of land forms, its creepy critters, and its stillness in contrast to the churning of the ocean.

50. At the beach we tend to get our priorities in order, because we have time to think and pray. God meets us there and blesses us in so many ways.

51. The possibility of hurricane evacuation forces us to be in a readiness/preparedness state. Just to ponder the possibility makes the adrenaline flow with excitement and a sense of adventure. Shouldn't the expectation of Jesus' return and our evacuation to our eternal home elicit that same response?

52. A no-tan line around my wrist is one of my favorite sea treasures. Only my "biological clock" nudges me to leave her shores for nourishment or sleep.

53. The ocean, like God's own spirit, is like a magnet which draws us back time and time again, and each time we return, we wonder why we ever left.

54. Leaving the sea is such "sweet sorrow." I live to return to her, and that makes life worth living. We should experience that same emotion after being in the presence of our Lord.

55. No one is impressed by designer labels at the beach.

56. Some of my most precious sea treasures are those given without reservation by others. Like my cobalt blue sea glass from a Kentucky vacationer, the favored tiny raspberry colored shells given joyfully by a small child, and the majority of my sharks' teeth which I have yet to develop the knack of finding.

57. It's fun to teach others a bit about an island I've come to love. I like to share from my daily bounty of sea treasures, especially with the kiddos, and I delight in seeing their eyes light up! It is better to give than receive. We should be willing and honored to give away a bit of what we've learned from experience about our Creator to those passing by who may not know Him. They take away something real to hold on to like the shell in their pocket. We receive a bit of joy unspeakable.

58. One piece bathing suits would beautify the beach environment, but, hey, with all God's beauty surrounding them, whose going to notice my bikini? To quote Popeye, "I yam what I yam, and that's all that I yam!"

"I'm okay, you're okay. We're all okay."

59. Bathing suit beauties in all our glory!

The Girls

Beach trips with the family remain in our memory more than many other vacations, down to the matching red and white striped bathing suits seen in the above picture.

60. Coffee tastes better at the beach because you don't have to hurry through it, and you savor every sip.

61. Not using a hair dryer for a whole weekend is a treasure.

62. Beach survival tools include a hat, shades, sunscreen, and deodorant.

63.   Sharing the beach with your friends should come with a warning: beach bum is contagious.

64.   As a beach bum, age and sun spots are par for the course.

65. As we read in the book of Genesis, in the beginning God created the ocean and all the sea creatures, and then He said it was good, amen. We agree.

66. God's promises are worth more than the leprechaun's gold at the end of the rainbow.

67. You feel rich when you find a sand dollar.

68. Confucius say, "He who leaves flip-flops on the water's edge at high tide say Bye-Bye to his flops."

69. To be truly happy, be a "Son" worshipper.

70. "At that time men will see the Son of Man coming in clouds with great power and glory." Mark 13:26 (NIV)

"Darkness into Light" painting by Edna Roeder 912-441-0107 [14]

"Sing to God, sing praise to His name, extol Him who rides on the clouds – His name is the Lord – and rejoice before Him." Psalm 68:4 (NIV)

71. When the waves pack a punch and have the power to knock you on your fanny, it helps to have a hand to hold. True during life's turmoils, too.

"For I am the Lord your God, who churns up the sea so that its waves roar – the Lord Almighty is his name. I have put my words in your mouth and covered you with the shadow of my hand." Psalm 51:15-16a (NIV)

72. Children run into the arms of their dad despite the fact he's standing in the unknown ocean depths which without his presence would be frightening. Their unwavering trust in a father who cares for them with every ounce of his being is so evident as you watch their playful interactions. We have an Abba Father who gave His life for us as our eternal lifeguard, so we wouldn't drown in our sins. No one has ever done that before. How could I not have childlike faith in a superhero like that?

73. "The ocean stirs the heart, inspires the imagination and brings eternal joy to the soul." Wyland

74. "Then God said, 'Let us make man in our image, in our likeness, and let them rule over the fish of the sea and the birds of the air, over the livestock, over all the earth, and over all the creatures that move along the ground.'" Genesis 1:26 (NIV)

Photographed by Barbara Ellliott[15]

This scripture is much more of a compliment to my cousin than my comment that he resembled "The Old Man and the Sea."

"Egret" by Edna Roeder 912-441-0107[16]

75. "We can't direct the wind, but we can adjust the sails. For maximum happiness, peace, and contentment, may we choose a positive attitude." Thomas S. Monson

Photo during a storm on Amelia Island by Carrie Viohl[17]

76. May we weather life's storms like the palm tree withstands hurricane-strength gusts. The palm's strong root system is imperative to anchor her. Her tall, thin trunk is flexible when displaced by forceful winds. Her palm fronds reach higher and higher and produce nourishment for the entire tree. Are our feet on solid ground? Are we rigid or flexible with life's changes? Do we reach to the highest Provider of spiritual nourishment? No wonder we topple over like a corn stalk when the winds are stirred by a sneeze.

Cooper's Town, Abaco, Bahamas by Anthony M. Moser, M.D. moosem@colquittregional.com[18]

"Give me the sun and the sea and a little spot on the sand just for me." Author Unknown

77. "The righteous will flourish like a palm tree, they will grow like a cedar of Lebanon; planted in the house of the Lord, they will flourish in the courts of our God. They will still bear fruits in their old age, they will stay fresh and green, proclaiming, 'The Lord is upright; he is my Rock, and there is no wickedness in him.'" Psalm 92:12-15 (NIV)

78. We have not because we ask not. God wants to give us the desires of our hearts and is a good Father. I'd looked all weekend for my "sought after" sea glass and was hesitant to go inland after a dry run. I prayed for just one sparkly gem. I immediately found green glass, then brown, then clear, one after another to total five pieces. What an awesome God!

79. Serendipitous sea treasures frequently appear when least expected, when we're not even looking for them. We're amazed that this gift appears right in front of our eyes. Don't forget to say thank you.

80. People smile more at the beach.

Annie Clymer Coleman[19]

81. I believe I want to increase my salt intake!

82. Beach people are healthier, mentally and physically.

83. As the coxswain for Girls Crew Team at Bolles High School in Jacksonville, Florida, my seventeen year old niece, Lainey Harris, helped her team achieve third place overall in the Florida State Championship.

Photos of Girls Crew Team, Bolles High School, Jacksonville, Florida, used by permission of Jan Olson, Senior Director of Communications & Marketing.[20]

84. "We are tied to the ocean. And when we go back to the sea, whether it is to sail or to watch – we are going back from whence we came." John F. Kennedy (1917-1963)

"Twenty years from now, you'll be more disappointed by the things you didn't do, than by the ones you did do. So throw off the bowlines. Sail away from the safe harbor. Catch the trade winds in your sails." Mark Twain (1835-1910)

85. Beach mentality is real. Life is slower, whether vacationing or living as a local.

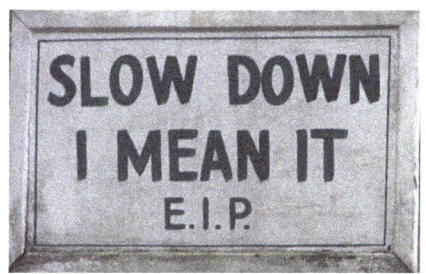

86. "Have I dreamt I am a mermaid…Or am I a mermaid dreaming I am me?" Emily Schoenfeld

Explore your inner mermaid

87. "Go, eat your food with gladness, and drink your wine with a joyful heart, for God favors what you do." Ecclesiastes 9:7 (NIV)

"Life is what you make it. Always has been. Always will be." Grandma Moses (Anna Mary Robertson Moses 1860-1961)

88. My sand bucket is always half full at the beach, never half empty.

89. Never say "goodbye" to the ocean; just say "see ya later."

90. "I've got ocean devotion!" Unknown Author

91. Beach walks result in that all-over tan. You are never streaky.

92. There's less wear and tear on a beach house because you're rarely there.

93. While standing in line to make a purchase at a coastal shop, it tickled my fancy to spy sand-crusted, sandaled feet. I felt a common bond of beach brotherhood.

94. "The sand between my toes. The water washes away my woes." Author Unknown

95. You forget to eat at the beach. Great diet plan.

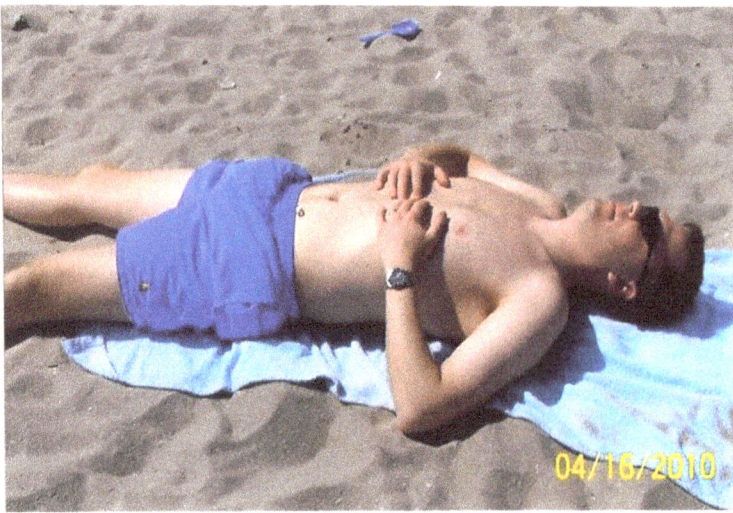

Why does a tan make you feel like you look healthier? Gives your face a shiny glow!

96. I would have flunked the course in finding sharks' teeth. My excuse was that I walked too fast, or I didn't have enough patience, or my eyes just don't discriminate the glossy, black, triangular shapes from broken black shell impostors, or it hurts my back to bend over so long to search. Well, I'm reformed. Recently I've slowed my pace, and by digging at the right spot, the extra effort has paid off. The sharp sharks' canines can be found. Doesn't take a knack, just effort. Now that I've conquered my doubt, I'm driven to possess more and more. I wait to fill a glass vessel to display my bounty. I've met many sharks' teeth seekers who even pray for abundance. Hey, whatever will get you to pray. We should be as diligent about delving into God's word which is sharper than any two-edged sword or shark's tooth. Yea, there are lots of imposters, but when you grab hold of the real thing, you know it. Then, you become passionate about wanting more and more. You want to fill your vessel to overflowing, so the world will see the truth.

97. May the Son penetrate your being and warm you with his love.

98. Bicycles are a preferred mode of transportation at the beach.

99. At the beach, you're more daring to try unusual things like sushi and surfing (once before I turned fifty to freak out my kids). That's the same year I auditioned for the TV show, "The Bachelorette." Despite knowing I exceeded the age expectation, it was worth the whistles!

100. I make a joyful noise (could be interpreted as singing) more at the beach and when I'm "caught," I just keep on chirping.

101. Majestic palm trees sway with tropical breezes and invite you to dance to the rhythm of the waves' percussion.

102. I didn't volunteer for Fear Factor, but a snake crossing the boardwalk does qualify. Why did the chicken cross the board walk? Because that's the only way to retrieve my car keys! After a complimentary strawberry daiquiri, I was accompanied by a brave Ritz Carlton employee with a shovel. I didn't forget my lifeguard training of 47 years ago. The "quick reverse" came in handy. It worked well when dating also.

103. Don't play with danger. My Florida State Farm Insurance Agent cautioned me against being on the beach when lightning approached, because more people in Florida are killed by lightning than by auto accidents. I decided not to hope for Ben Franklin's luck and to seek shelter. This was only after I waited out a storm, pouting, when the celestial fireworks began. It was my first memorable trip to the beach since moving to the island.

104. At the beach you notice clouds. God paints the sky to amaze us, and we generally don't even look up and notice His daily heavenly gifts. Forgive us, Lord. My granddaughter, Ava, told me when she was five years of age that the moon, stars, and Jesus give her peace. "They go with me wherever I go." From the mouth of babes.

105. Too much of a good thing at the beach isn't too much of a good thing.

106. At the beach daydreaming comes naturally.

"The only thing worth stealing is a kiss from a sleeping child." Joe Houldsworth

107. I love to dance the night away with my "stars" at Ziggy Mahoney's nightclub in St. Simons Island, Georgia.

"A girl's best friend is her mother." Anonymous

108. Our pets even enjoy a "holiday" at the islands. Dogs love to run on the beach with their masters. My Betsy V. Ross had rather lounge at the beach house feeling quite fashionable in her tropical ensemble.

109. "If it's not fun, forget it!"

The sweet mother of a pediatric patient whom I treated for many years gave me a button with that logo on it, because she knew that's how I structured my physical therapy sessions. I just happen to agree with the wisest man who has ever lived, King Solomon (970 to 931 BC). In Ecclesiastes 8:15 (NIV) he instructs, "So I commend the enjoyment of life, because nothing is better for a man under the sun than to eat and drink and be glad. Then joy will accompany him in his work all the days of the life God has given him under the sun."

"Coastal Living" isn't just a magazine but an entirely different way of life, full of joy, health, nature, and fun! Where else can you dress up in your pajamas the day after Thanksgiving to shop in Old Town, Amelia Island or don your flamingo Halloween costume to compete in a costume contest at the Ritz Carlton, Amelia Island?

No wonder I received my nickname, Jubilant Jennifer, while I lived on Amelia Island!

My wedding party

Sleeping Beauty and the Seven Dwarfs. I'm Mrs. Doc, of course. We had a blast even though we didn't win!

I want to be an Outrageous Old Woman
who will never be
called an old lady.
Maybe a little crazy,
but not lazy,
sharing love and
laughter
till the forever after.
Patsy Moore, 2007[21]

110.   On the island my favorite place is the Ritz.
There I can dress up in all my glitz.

I am treated like a queen
which makes me beam.

You can let go of your cares,
if you dare.

The staff is really sincere.
You can tell when they grin ear to ear!

They take the ordinary
and turn it into extraordinary!

Why have a mundane vacation
when you can experience such elation!

Rediscover fun,
in the sun,
with your hon.

You can dance
and make romance.

Refresh, renew,
and come unglued!

The spa services were a class act,
and that's a fact!

You create memories sweet,
that keep me on my feet.

During those "normal" days,
that often leave your mind in a haze.

But in a "twinkling of an eye,"
you don't even have to ask why.

My thoughts return to my sweet Amelia,
so far away,
I'll be back there someday.

God said in our work we are to excel,
and that you do super-duper swell !!!

With gratitude,
for your giving attitude.

JUMP

Myrtle Beach, S.C. by Edna Roeder 912-441-0107[22]

"Our Father in heaven! May your name be kept holy. May your Kingdom come, Your will be done on earth as in heaven…"Matthew 6:9-10 (Complete Jewish Bible)

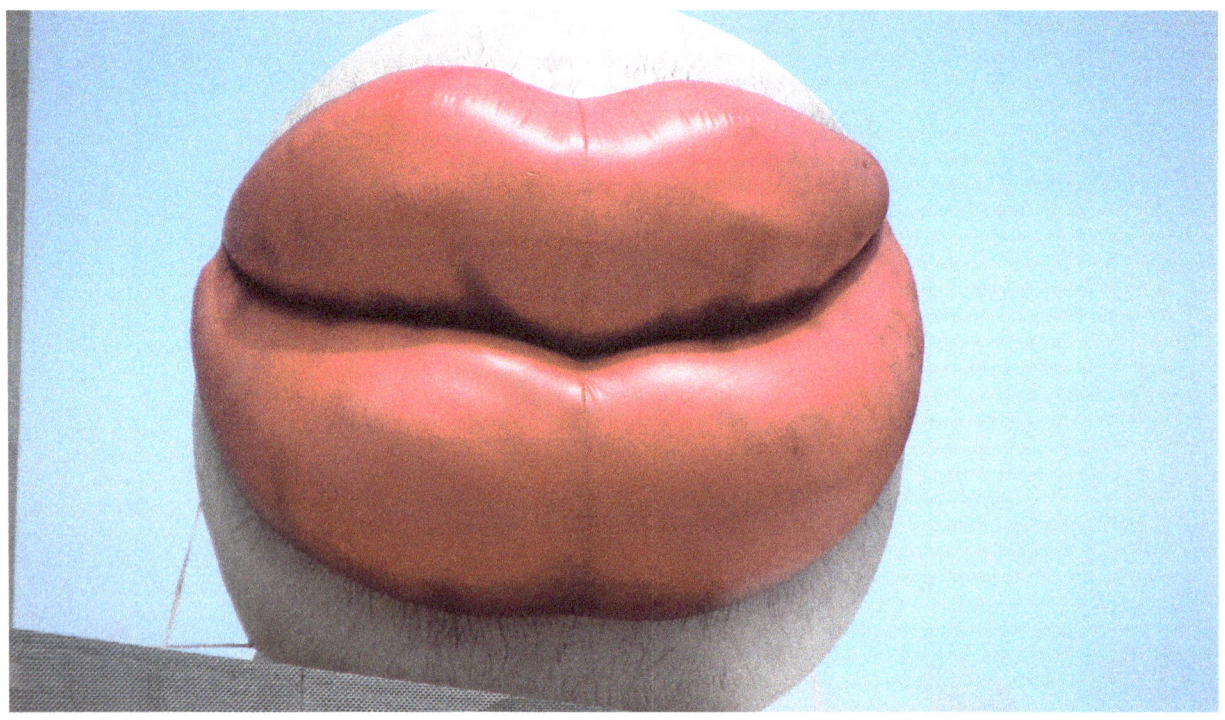

111. "Of all the commandments, which is the most important?"
"The most important one," answered Jesus, "is this: 'Hear, O Israel, the Lord our God, the Lord is one. Love the Lord your God with all your heart and with all your soul and with all your mind and with all your strength.' The second is this: 'Love your neighbor as yourself.' There is no commandment greater than these." Mark 12:28-31 (NIV)

"I, alone, cannot change the world, but I can cast a stone across the waters to create many ripples." Mother Teresa (1910-1997)

112. "We ourselves feel that what we are doing is just a drop in the ocean. But the ocean would be less because of that missing drop." Mother Teresa

"My life is a message." Mahatma Gandhi (1869-1948)

If your "drop of water in the ocean" was analyzed by the local pool maintenance service, what "life message" would it reveal? Is your life well balanced spiritually, mentally and physically or do you need to make adjustments?

"…that Christ died for our sins according to the Scriptures, that he was buried, that he was raised on the third day according to the Scriptures." 1 Corinthians 15:3-4 (NIV)

"My dear children I write this to you so that you will not sin. But if anybody does sin, we have one who speaks to the Father in our defense – Jesus Christ, the Righteous One. He is the atoning sacrifice of our sins and not only for ours but also for the sins of the whole world." 1 John 2:1-2 (NIV)

Rules for Doing Good
Do all the good you can,
In all the ways you can,
To all the people you can,
In every place you can,
At all the times you can,
As long as ever you can.
    John Wesley (1703-1791)

113. "Every good and perfect gift is from above, coming down from the Father of the heavenly lights, who does not change like shifting shadows." James 1:17 (NIV)

Beaufort, S.C. by Edna Roeda 912-441-0107[23]

"He has made everything beautiful in its time." Ecclesiastes 4:11 (NIV)

114. "Let us fix our eyes on Jesus, the author and perfector of our faith, who for the joy set before him endured the cross, scorning its shame, and sat down at the right hand of the throne of God." Hebrews 12:2 (NIV)

Easter Week, Beaufort, S. C. by Robert DeLoach 843-522-0263[24]

"May I never boast except in the cross of our Lord Jesus Christ…" Galatians 6:14 (NIV)

115. "The name of Adonai (the Lord) is a strong tower;
a righteous person runs to it and is raised high (above danger)."
Proverbs 18:10 (Complete Jewish Bible)

116. "Your word is a lamp to my feet and a light for my path." Psalm 119:105 (NIV)

117. "Trust in Adonai (the Lord) with all your heart;
do not rely on your own understanding.
In all your ways acknowledge him;
then he will level your paths."
Proverbs 3:5-6 (Complete Jewish Bible)

118. Jesus is the Bridge
      "Like a bridge over troubled water I will lay me down"[25]

      Right at the feet of his Father,
      Your Father if you accept his Son as your Lord and Savior.

      There is no other way.

   Jesus answered, "I am the way and the truth and the life.
No one comes to the Father except through me." John 14:6 (NIV)

119. Topless is for toddlers and convertibles.

"I don't say that we ought to all misbehave, but we ought to look as if we could!" Orson Welles

I totally agree!

A dream come true was a beach birthday wedding at the Ritz Carlton at Amelia Island.

"Shout To the Lord"

My Jesus, My Savior
Lord, there is none like You
All of my days
I want to praise
The wonders of Your mighty love.

My comfort, my shelter
Tower of refuge and strength

Let every breath, all that I am
Never cease to worship You.

Shout to the Lord
All the earth let us sing
Power and majesty, praise to the King
Mountains bow down and the seas will roar
At the sound of Your name.

I sing for joy at the work of Your hands,
Forever I'll love You,
Forever I'll stand,
Nothing compares to the promise I have
In You

"Shout to the Lord" by Darlene Zschech, Copyright © 1993 Wondrous Worship[26]

Ahoy! From Amelia Island, Florida. November 30, 2003

Blessings to the beach bum recipient of our message in a bottle!

We hope you can be a happy as we are this day. God will bless our union as husband and wife with our new life beginning on my 51st birthday (Jen), November 28, 2003. The width and depth of our love is as immense as the ocean blue and will be as constant as the ebb and flow of the tides. Just as we are drawn to the ocean, we are drawn to each other.

The days ahead are filled with as many opportunities as there are grains of sand on the beach. The waves can appear wild and furious or calm and peaceful. Just as in life, there can be a great sense of anticipation, excitement, peace and calm. No matter if blue skies or stormy sea, hand in hand we will walk life's beach together and we look forward to the journey. May we always find a shell in our pockets and sand in our shoes!!

God bless you, Duke and Jennifer Harris

"They say there are other fish in the sea, but honestly, you are the only one for me." Author Unknown

The Pelican

A wonderful bird is a pelican,
His beak will hold more than his belican.
He can take in his beak
Food enough for a week.
But I'm damned if I can see how the helican.

Dixon Lanier Merritt (1879–1972)[27]

My Kentucky granddaughter was barely walking,
  but when she toddled into the
  cold ocean you could hear her
  squawking!

Her sea legs didn't hold her up and she began to cry,
  and wondered why,
    her camera-clad Mimi and
    Mom just waved "Hi."

Her dad accused the paparazzi of neglect.
  Annie Clymer wondered where is
  the respect?

But we have her first ocean
experience as a Kodak moment to share,
  and that will show just how much
  we care!

JUMP

Tears
  in my ears,
    with fears,
      to leave Fernandina Beach.

But my heart will reach from Moultrie, Georgia, 190 miles
  with a gazillion smiles,
Of memories sweet
  that kept me on my feet,
Walking on the sand.
  God, this is such beautiful land!
I have such gratitude,
  for eight years to have been
  blessed with this longitude and latitude.
    It gave me a sunny attitude!
This is hard,
  to give up my yard.
But Father knows best.
  I'll forget worry and the rest.
I trust you.
  What else can I do?
Bye
  sky,
    sun and fun.
I'll play
  another day.
My Atlantic, my faithful friend,
  with God, your ear, you always did lend.
    I wish our time together I could extend.
Parting is such sweet sorrow.
  In my dreams. I'll see you tomorrow!

Your beach buddy, Jen
(Written 11-21-09 after selling home at Amelia Island, Florida)

So much time has elapsed since I visited Amelia Island, which I love so dearly. It seems like an eternity.

Time is
Too Slow for those who Wait,
Too Swift for those who Fear,
Too Long for those who Grieve,
Too Short for those who Rejoice;
But for those who Love,
Time is not.

Henry Van Dyke (1852-1933)[28]

My Morning Prayer

Thank you, Lord, for sleep so sweet
  That helps to keep me on my feet.

In your will I want to stay.
  Protect me, Lord, throughout the day.

I will be your hands and feet
  To anyone I chance to meet.

Help me grow
  So I can show,
    So many lost the way to go.

I love you, Lord, I hope you see,
  I'm glad you died to set me free!
                                    Amen.
                                    JUMP

King David's Morning Prayer

Let the morning bring me word
of your unfailing love,
    For I have put my trust in you.
Show me the way I should go,
    For I hide myself in you.
Teach me to do your will,
    For you are my God,
      may your good Spirit
        lead me on level ground.
For your name's sake, O Lord,
    Preserve my life;
      In your righteousness, bring me out
        of trouble.
In your unfailing love, silence my enemies;
    Destroy all my foes,
      For I am your servant.
                    Psalm 143:8-12 (NIV)

Exiled

Searching my heart for its true sorrow,
   This is the thing I find to be:
That I am weary of words and people,
   Sick of the city, wanting the sea;

Wanting the sticky, salty sweetness
   Of the strong wind and shattered spray;
Wanting the loud sound and the soft sound
   Of the big surf that breaks all day.

Always before about my dooryard,
   Marking the reach of the winter sea,
Rooted in sand and dragging drift-wood,
   Straggled the purple sweet-pea;

Always I climbed the wave at morning,
   Shook the sand from my shoes at night,
That now am caught beneath great buildings,
   Stricken with noise, confused with light.

If I could hear the green piles groaning
   Under the windy wooden piers,
See once again the bobbing barrels,
   And the black sticks that fence the weirs,

If I could see the weedy mussels
   Crusting the wrecked and rotting hulls,
Hear once again the hungry crying
   Overhead, of the wheeling gulls,

Feel once again the shanty straining
        the turning of the
Fear once again the rising freshet,
        Dread the bell in the fog outside,

I should be happy, -- that was happy
        All day long on the coast of Maine!
I have a need to hold and handle
        Shells and anchors and ships again!

I should be happy, that am happy
        Never at all since I came here.
I am too long away from water.
        I have a need of water near.

Edna St. Vincent Millay[29]

"Save me, O God,
for the waters have come up to my neck.
I sink in the miry depths,
where there is no foothold." Psalm 69:1-2 (NIV)

"The engulfing waters threatened me, the deep surrounded me…" Jonah 2:5 (NIV)

"…all your waves and breakers have swept over me." Psalm 42:7 (NIV)

"…You have overwhelmed me with all your waves." Psalm 88:7 (NIV).

"From the ends of the earth I call to you,
I call as my heart grows faint;
lead me to the rock that is higher than I." Psalm 61:2 (NIV)

"Reach down your hand from on high;
deliver me and rescue me
from the mighty waters," Psalm 144:7(NIV)

"He reached down from on high and took hold of me;
he drew me out of deep waters." Psalm 18:16 (NIV)

"Thunderclap" photographed by Steve Vaughn[30]

"He brought me out into a spacious place;

he rescued me because he delighted in me." Psalm 18:19 (NIV)

"For who is God besides the LORD?

And who is the Rock except our God?" Psalm 18:31 (NIV)

"Be my rock of refuge, to which I can always go;" Psalm 71:3 (NIV)

"Truly my soul finds rest in God;

my salvation comes from him.

Truly he is my rock and my salvation;

he is my fortress, I will never be shaken." Psalm 62:1-2 (NIV)

"I will exalt you, LORD,

for you lifted me out of the depths…" PSALM 30:1 (NIV)

"He stilled the storm to a whisper;

the waves of the sea were hushed.

They were glad when it grew calm,

and he guided them to their desired haven." Psalm 107:29-30 (NIV)

Photo by Lainey Harris[31]

"Oceans (Where Feet May Fail)" by Hillsong[32]

This song was sung at the funeral of Bill Edwards and is included in memory of Bill and in honor of his wife Bonnie. They met in the eighth grade and were happily married for 52 years. Bill and Bonnie depended on Christ even more as they battled Bill's cancer for thirteen years. "Oceans" was one of their favorite songs that they listened to every night before bedtime. Bonnie considered the words "a commitment to do what it says."

You call me out upon the waters
The great unknown where feet may fail
And there I find You in the mystery
In oceans deep
My faith will stand

And I will call upon Your name
And keep my eyes above the waves
When oceans rise
My soul will rest in Your embrace
For I am Yours and You are mine

Your grace abounds in deepest waters
Your sovereign hand
Will be my guide
Where feet may fail and fear surrounds me
You've never failed and You won't start now

So I will call upon Your name
And keep my eyes above the waves
When oceans rise
My soul will rest in Your embrace
For I am Yours and You are mine

Spirit lead me where my trust is without borders
Let me walk upon the waters
Wherever You would call me
Take me deeper than my feet could ever wander
And my faith will be made stronger
In the presence of my Savior

Oh, Jesus, you're my God!

I will call upon Your name
Keep my eyes above the waves
My soul will rest in Your embrace
I am Yours and You are mine

The Lighthouse©jean-guichard.com[33]

Life is not measured by the number of breaths we take,
but by the number of moments that take our breath away.
Anonymous

About the Author

Jennifer Clymer Harris has lived in Moultrie, Georgia, for fifteen years with her husband, a South Georgia gentleman physician with a real southern drawl and their three rescue cats. She is an avid "Blue-to-the bone" Kentucky Wildcat fan in Georgia Bull Dawg Country. She proudly drives her UK - stickered "catmobile" displaying her pride. Jennifer has enjoyed her profession of physical therapy for thirty-three years, specializing in pediatrics for much of her career. Jennifer is most in her happy place when she's digging in the dirt to beautify her "pooltanical" garden and even swims when her flowers are well tended. As well, Bible study is a constant and consistent joy because it has been essential to her growth in the Lord. Oddly enough, she claims prison ministry with Bill Glass Champions for Life/Behind the Walls makes for a fun weekend! Dancing and grandbabies are her passion; you can't get better than dancing with your grandbabies! She has three granddaughters, Annie, Ava, Madelynn (Touie), and two grandsons, Clay and Malkolm. Jennifer has collected dolls since her daughter was a child, thus releasing the little girl inside who loves dolls. To renew her child-like spirit she mentors in the Colquitt County school system, volunteers in multiple summer kid's day camps, and teaches kindergarten Sunday School at Heritage Church. Visiting friends in local nursing homes has been a big part of her life.

Book produced by, WestBow Press, A DIVISION OF THOMAS NELSON &
ZONDERVAN (Angela Smitman, PUBLISHING CONSULTANT)

Endnotes

1. Scripture quotations marked (NIV) are taken from the Holy Bible, New International Version®, NIV®. Copyright © 1973, 1978, 1984, 2011 by Biblica, Inc.™ Used by permission of Zondervan. All rights reserved worldwide. www.zondervan.com The "NIV" and "New International Version" are trademarks registered in the United States Patent and Trademark Office by Biblica, Inc.™

2. *"Johnny Lingo's Eight-Cow Wife" by Patricia McGerr. © 1965 by Patricia McGerr (1917–1985), First published in Woman's Day. Reprinted in* Reader's Digest, February 1988, pp138-141 (ISBN 0939184613)

3. Scripture quotations marked (Complete Jewish Bible) Used by permission of Messianic Jewish Publishers, 6120 Day Long Lane, Clarksville, MD 21029. www.messianicjewish.net.

4. *"She Who Loves the Beach"* art and poetry © Suzy Toronto, www.suzytoronto.com. Used by permission.

5. *"Kissed by the Sun"* by Doug Cavanah. Used by permission.

6. "Benched Beach Basket of Treasures," by Rhonda McEnroe www.ENROE.studio.com 270-993-2282. Used by permission.

7. "Frolic" painting by Danny Phifer. Used by permission.

8. *Merriam-Webster's Collegiate Dictionary, © 1974 by G. & C. Merriam Co., Previous edition copyright © 1973 by G. & C. Merriam Co.*

9. Drawing on page 24 by Annie Clymer Coleman.

10. Photo by Sandra Morrison, Amelia Island, Florida. Used by permission.

11. Painting by Hannah Haunte, Age 8. Used by permission.

12. Photo by Edna Roeder 912-441-0107. Used by permission.

13. Photo by Valerie Tipton. Used by permission.

14. "Darkness into Light" painting by Edna Roeder 912-441-0107. Used by permission.

15. Photographed by Barbara Ellliott. Used by permission.

16. "Egret" by Edna Roeder 912-441-0107. Used by permission.

17. Photo during a storm on Amelia Island by Carrie Viohl. Used by permission.

18. Cooper's Town, Abaco, Bahamas by Anthony M. Moser, M.D. moosem@colquittregional.com. Used by permission.

19. Drawing on page 58 by Annie Clymer Coleman.

20. Photos of Girls Crew Team, Bolles High School, Jacksonville, Florida, used by permission of Jan Olson, Senior Director of Communications and Marketing.

21. "I want to be an Outrageous Old Woman" card by Patsy Moore. Used by permission.

22. Myrtle Beach, S.C. by Edna Roeder 912-441-0107. Used by permission.

23. Beaufort, S.C. by Edna Roda 912-441-0107. Used by permission.

24. Easter Week, Beaufort, S. C. by Robert DeLoach 843-522-0263. Used by permission.

25. "Bridge Over Troubled Water" ©Universal Music Publishing Group. Written by Paul Simon and released by Simon and Garfunkel, January, 1970.

26. "Shout to the Lord" by Darlene Zschech, Copyright © 1993 Wondrous Worship (Administered by Music Services o/b/o Llano Music LLC) All rights reserved. Used by permission. License No. 545512.

27. Merritt, Dixon Lanier (1879–1972) "The Pelican" penned in 1910 Ratiocinativa website https://ratiocinativa.wordpress.com/2013/07/13/the-pelican-dixon-lanier-merritt/ August 10, 2015 The Pelican, in Nashville Banner 22 April 1913.

28. Van Dyke, Henry – *Time Is* from *Treasured Poems that Touch the Heart* by Mary Sanford Laurence (p. 47) (1996).

29. Millay, Edna St. Vincent – *Exiled*, *Poems of the Sea*, selected and edited by J. D. McClatchy, Alfred A. Knopf, c Everyman's Library (2001). Used with permission.

30. "Thunderclap" photographed by Steve Vaughn. Used by permission.

31. Photo by Lainey Harris. Used by permission.

32. "Oceans (Where Feet May Fail)", written by Joel Houston, Matt Crocker, Salomon Lighthelm, Song ID: 67604, Copyright 2013 Hillsong Music Publishing (APRA) (adm. In the US and Canada at CapitolCMGPublishing.com) All rights reserved. Used by permission. License No. 573769.

33. "The Lighthouse" photograph by Jean Guichard ©jean-guichard.com. Used by permission.

34. Commissioned beach painting by Kathy Nelson, Colquitt County Art Center.

Attempts were made through several search engines to acknowledge and credit all original authors of quotes and to obtain permission. Many quips in this collection were plaques or signs with no origin posted.

Kathy Nelson, Colquitt County Arts Center[34]

After reading Beach Reflections, please share any feedback through my email (jumpharris@gmail.com). Thank you for spending your time reading Beach Reflections, as it has become so much a part of me!